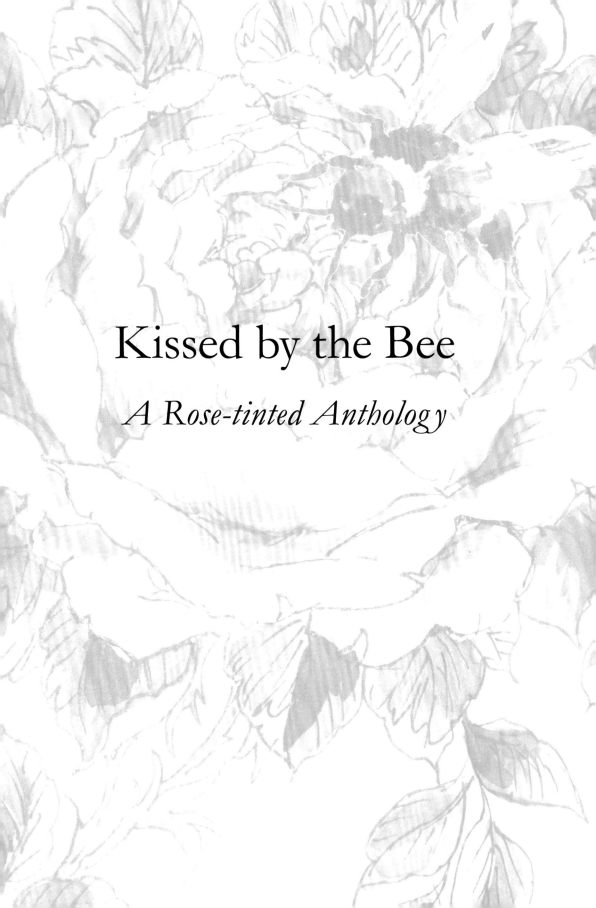

Kissed by the Bee

A Rose-tinted Anthology

Kissed by the Bee

A Rose-tinted Anthology

Maureen Melvin

Illustrations
Raphilena Bonito

TRICORN
BOOKS

Kissed by the Bee
A Rose-tinted Anthology
Maureen Melvin

Design © 131 Design Ltd
www.131design.org
Text © Maureen Melvin
Illustrations © Raphilena Bonito

ISBN 978-0-9573435-6-6
A CIP catalogue record for this book is available from the British Library.

Published 2013 by Tricorn Books
131 High Street, Old Portsmouth
PO1 2HW
www.tricornbooks.co.uk

Printed & bound in UK

Also by Maureen Melvin,
with illustrations by Geoff Crook:

Paws For Thought
Paws Again
Paws For Pasta
Paws Forever
Paws For Shakespeare

Remembering my mother

Nora Melvin

A dedicated gardener

Acknowledgements

W.S. Gilbert for the title from "*Ruddigore*"
by Gilbert and Sullivan.

Michael Marriott, technical director at David Austin
Roses Ltd., who led me to the history of *Sombreuil*.

A.E. Housman from "A Shropshire Lad" LIV.

Back cover photograph Sarah Burnell.

Contents

A Yorkshire Garden

My mother loved her garden, she gardened all her life
When not involved with children or the duties of a wife.
Though nurtured in the sunny South her future lay elsewhere,
Transplanted by her husband to the smoke-filled Yorkshire air.

A bride of only nineteen years, superlatively matched,
She learned to run a doctor's house with surgery attached.
By purest chance this fertile patch held all her gardening needs
Within "The Rhubarb Triangle" 'twixt Wakefield town and Leeds.

A privet hedge was planted round the edges of the grounds
Small trees soon rose above it, shooting up by leaps and bounds.
A tennis court was laid to grass, a fallow field was tilled
Where vegetables could flourish, leaving room for her to build
The greenhouse she had longed for where this youthful connoisseur
Pricked out the seeds and nursed the plants which always bloomed for her.

A border for her favourite flowers curved down below the drive
Beside a bed of roses which were lucky to survive
My father's intervention with his amputating knife
And nervous blossoms hung their heads and trembled for their life.

There raspberry canes were thickly hung with ripe and luscious fruit
And I could hide and stuff myself, with cook in hot pursuit,
Chasing me with a pudding bowl, she knew where I had gone,
My task to single out the best for dinner later on.

I've tasted raspberries far and wide wherever there's a chance,
Occasionally in Scotland and more frequently in France.
Huge berries in the USA and tiny ones in Rome
And nowhere were they half as good as those we grew at home.

Still nothing lasts forever even raspberries disappear
Though few have faced a coup de grâce like those remembered here.
My father, armed with garden shears, (my mother not around)
Went mad among the raspberry canes and razed them to the ground.

When charged with this barbarity he blustered, "Have no fear
I've only cut them back a bit just wait until next year!"
Through June, July and August too we waited, but in vain,
The berries we had loved so well were never seen again.

But this was long ago and now my mother is not there,
I wish I'd paid attention about what to grow and where.
It strikes me, as I stand perplexed before some wilting tree,
How sad it is her expertise was not passed down to me.

Cotswold Collection

Flower Arranging

I once lived in a garden – with a house – near Tunbridge Wells
With shady trees and winding paths and little leafy dells
There were scores of rhododendrons with important Latin names
And camellias and azaleas and things that grew in frames.

A huge herbaceous border filled with pansies, pinks and phlox
With peonies in profusion and delphiniums and stocks
There were strawberry beds and raspberry canes and rabbits out of bounds
And a cottage for the gardener in a comer of the grounds.

I did the flowers on Thursday – a day I came to dread
For the trials and tribulations and the turbulence ahead.
I washed out all the vases and I filled them to the brim
Then I packed them tight with chicken wire and taped it round the rim.

The gardener brought me armfuls of the things he thought I'd like
For I never picked a flower myself in case he went on strike.
He gathered boughs of greenery and sprays of silvery shrubs
And he left them, drinking deeply, by the door in wooden tubs.

You need a tall, well balanced branch to regulate the height
A graceful frond towards the left, another to the right.
The scaffolding is now in place but do not turn your head
Or you' ll find it facing back to front and left to right instead.

That hurdle safely over, you are well into your stride
Putting larger flowers in the centre and the small ones at the side
And when you add the final touch, one perfect peony more
The whole thing topples over and goes crashing to the floor.

We went away to France, one year, to miss the summer showers,
The gardener's wife consoled the dog, the gardener did the flowers
And when I viewed his handiwork, it wasn't hard to see
I'd been harbouring an expert who was twice as good as me.

Thereafter, on a Thursday, I absconded for the day
The hairdresser, a ladies lunch, perhaps a matinee
Returning through the dusky lanes past pheasant, fox and mouse
To a softly scented garden and a fragrant flower-filled house.

And now I live in Gloucestershire encased in Cotswold stone
With a little cottage garden which I manage on my own
We've built some very dry stone walls and planted lots of flowers
And I've started writing poems which keeps me occupied for hours.

The trouble with the writing is that time flies by so fast
And when I'm entertaining friends, the flowers are left 'til last
I fix the joint, the homemade soup, my soufflé, face and hair
Then nip outside at zero hour and strip the garden bare.

But wait! I have the answer to my flower arranging fears
Dried flowers may be expensive but they last for years and years.
They never swing from back to front or sway from side to side
My arrangements are spectacular and always cut and dried.

Now when I tour my garden with the secateurs in hand
The flowers no longer look away, I think they understand
I'm only just 'dead-heading', I don't pick them any more
And my roses ramble wildly round my Cotswold cottage door.

The Old Rose and the Young Rose

The old rose nodded gracefully
From high above the wall,
She was crimson, dark and beautiful
And loved by one and all.

Her perfume filled the garden
She was known for miles around
And she scarcely saw the little rose
Beneath her on the ground.

The young rose caught her eye and said
"I don't know what to do
I take my fertilizer
And my pesti-cider too.

I just grow green and round and fat
However hard I try
I want to have those big red blooms
That reach up to the sky."

The old rose looked down sadly
At the young one far below
"I remember at your age," she said
"Things do seem rather slow.

But then, you see, when I was young
It wasn't like today,
They dug a hole and planted you
And then they went away.

The air was pure, the wind was fresh
The rain was soft and clean
No chemicals were needed
For the horticultural scene.

There was no deep pollution then
No radio-active dust
No foul contamination
To inhale with every gust.

And in this new endangered world
They don't know how you feel
And they think they ought to feed you
When you do not need a meal.

One thing you must remember
When the gardener comes to spray,
Draw in your skirts, close up your mouth
And turn your head away."

"Oh, thank you," said the little rose,
"I'm sure you must be right
And when the gardener visits me
I'll fold my petals tight.

I'11 hang my head between my leaves
And when I feel the spray,
I'll hold my breath and shut my eyes
And look the other way.

And then if I behave myself,
One day, perhaps, who knows,
I might become a champion
And a Numero Uno rose."

The older rose felt drowsy
As she watched a petal fall
And she smiled a little smugly
Leaning back against the wall.

For she knew her roots were buried
Far beyond the reach of man
With his plant food and his spray gun
And his lethal watering can.

Mrs. Miller's Garden

"Now THAT's how daffodils should look!"
Oh – not that speech again,
I hear it every morning
When I drive him to the train.

My daffodils are tall and thin
And few and far between
They're rather short on yellow
But they've put on lots of green.

Now, Mrs. Miller's daffodils
Are something to behold.
They stand erect in serried ranks
A splash of Springtime gold.

Don't get me wrong, I love the Spring
There's just one thing I hate,
That cavalcade of daffodils
By Mrs. Miller's gate.

She's always in the garden
Whether it rains or snows
Of course, she's got green fingers
And I bet she's got green toes.

Her rockery descends in layers
And laps the country lane
No slug would dare to linger there
They're all in my domain.

She brought me trays of perfect plants
I wedged them side by side
It wasn't me that killed them off
They just lay down and died.

You can't be good at everything
No matter how you try
There's never been a problem
With my steak and kidney pie.

My garden quietly bides its time
From January to June
When roses crowd my cottage walls
And passers-by will swoon.

Although my efforts now bear fruit
He does not beg my pardon
Still, for a while. I don't hear much
Of Mrs. Miller's garden.

But Winter lies in wait and Spring
Is hiding in the hills
And bigger, better, brighter yet
Those blasted daffodils.

Before he starts his song of praise
I'm going to queer his pitch
I'll dig 'em up at dead of night
And chuck 'em in the ditch!

Captive in a Cotswold Garden

The insect, bug or arthropod
Like all good creatures hails from God.
Earwig, how come you were designed
To cause such chaos for mankind.

Could He who sees the sparrow fall
Have sent you here to plague us all,
To slither on your slimy tum
From dahlia to chrysanthemum?

Feasting on leaves and buds by night
And in the morning, out of sight
To slumber through the summer's day
Curled in the petals of your prey.

The honeysuckle wild and tall
Conceals the tank beside the wall
With perspex pipe and gauge, to show
Whether the oil is high or low.

Into this tempting tube one night
Antennae waving, eyes alight
The earwig comes to check the spoil
And fuel himself on heating oil.

Once down inside the narrow spout
He has no chance of climbing out
And finding that his hopes are sunk
Remains perpetually drunk.

The earwigs race from far and wide
To mount a rescue from inside:
He does not care, he feels no pain
And bends the elbow once again.

The boarding party soon perceives
There's more to life than stripping leaves
No need to tread the humble soil
When there's a chance of striking oil.

So down they scuttle, one by one,
And tumble in to join the fun
Careless of what the Fates may hold
They steep themselves in liquid gold.

Earwig, though you are not my friend
I pity your untimely end
Preserved in thrall 'til Kingdom-come
Still pickled in petroleum.

The Little Plant Pot

I'm a tiny little terracotta plant pot
And I stand about three inches from the ground
I spent all my early years
In the potting-shed in tears
For the gardener never wanted me around.

It is fair to say I'm not a thing of beauty
Ill-proportioned and unsteady on my base
I was never put to use
I became a real recluse
And the only empty plant pot in the place.

Occasionally I rolled into the garden
To be jeered at by a vulgar, modem urn
Disrespectful and sarcastic
He was only made of plastic
And he couldn't tell a plant pot from a churn.

One day when she was planting out for summer
The gardener saw me sulking by the shed
She examined me for size
Then to my immense surprise
"I know just what I can do with you," she said.

She washed me with the hosepipe from the greenhouse
And I sunbathed on the step 'til I was dry
Then with potash, loam and peat
I was practically complete
And she said I was a pleasure to the eye.

She set me on the terrace by the sundial
Where everyone could see me as they passed
With a fragile plant to treasure
I was happy beyond measure
And I knew I was acceptable at last.

She watered me each evening when the sun set
And my Bizzie Lizzie blossomed like a bride
We were quite a sight to see
She was twice as tall as me
And my terracotta heart was filled with pride.

Then August came and holidays were looming
And the gardener packed her case and caught the tide
No one ever stopped to think
We were desperate for a drink
And my Bizzie Lizzie withered, drooped and died.

When the gardener reappeared I thought she'd fire me
I was scared of being banished to the shed
But she said it was a shame
And that I was not to blame
So I wound up on the greenhouse shelf instead.

And now I'm used for annual propagation
In a category known as 'potting-on'
I coerce a callow seedling
With affection warmth and wheedling
'Til it changes from a duckling to a swan.

In summer time I day-dream in a seed box
And watch the young tomatoes turning red
There are rabbits passing through
For a lettuce leaf or two
And the spiders spin the scandal overhead.

I think about my exile to the wood-shed
And how miserable I was to be so small
But at last I realise
That whatever shape and size
There's a time and place and purpose for us all.

Class Distinction

I arrived in the rain on the morning train
With the scent of Spring in the air
They had wrapped my roots in plastic boots
And labelled me "Rose – With Care".

I was planted out and without a doubt
My quarters were quite the best
A substantial spread in a private bed
By a wall facing South. South West.

There were Chinese jars and a Versailles vase
But mine was a big round tub
On my left was a rose with a turned-up nose
On my right stood a flowering shrub.

I slept and I grew as the March winds blew
And the sunshine warmed my heart
By mid-July I was three feet high
And Life was about to start.

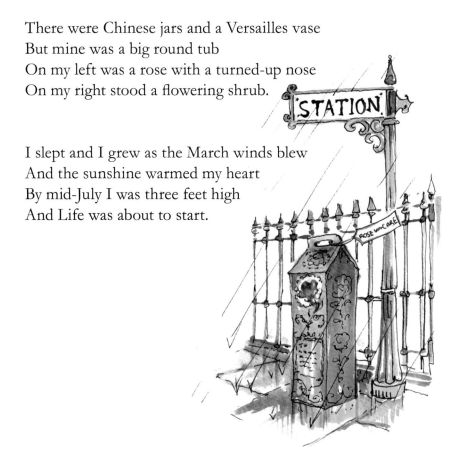

For the rose I had spurned, like the worm, had turned
Overnight into belle of the ball
In a pink-tipped dream of peach and cream
She flirted against the wall.

My heart was ablaze as she met my gaze
And I brushed her cheek with mine
But she laughed in my face at my bold embrace
And complained I was out of line.

Then a friendly breeze who was keen to please
Endeavoured to fan the flame
For a moment's bliss she was mine to kiss
Then she hung her head in shame.

Discretion fled and I crushed her head
In my arms – but she made no sound
I had loved too well and her petals fell
In a flutter of pink to the ground.

I was tied with twine to a wise old vine
Who pondered my sad disgrace
He would preach for hours on the ways of flowers
And he taught me to know my place.

I was out of my class when I made a pass
At my love, who was not to be,
For I was only a climbing rose
And she was a Hybrid Tea.

Oral Floral

"**I** wish I knew what ails you,"
Said the gardener to the rose.
"You forget you almost drowned me
With that crazy garden hose."

"You've had fertiliser, compost
And I spray you every week."
"No wonder I'm a nervous wreck
And too choked up to speak."

"I talk to you." "You said it friend,
That's half the blooming trouble.
Cut out those pearls of wisdom
And I'll blossom at the double."

"Perhaps you need a boyfriend."
"Ah, well, now you're talking sense.
I'm having drinks at sundown
With that climber on the fence!"

DRINKS AT SUNDOWN

Tales from a Hampshire Garden

Pigeons on the Piste

Though you plighted your troth in a garden
You have to find somewhere to live
Not Estate Agent's gems like a boat on the Thames
Which will probably leak like a sieve.

No, you go for a flat which is perfect
A tidy wee love nest for two.
Then your children arrive and when two become five
Your diminutive pad will not do.

It is time for the house and the garden
The dog and the field and the pool.
But the years fly away and you're faced with the day
When the boys are all boarding at school.

When the family home is deserted
You' re back in the market for two.
But persistent Old Age keeps on clearing the stage
Then there's only one left – and it's you.

So I searched for a refuge and found one
Though grandchildren made it seem small.
A conservatory tacked on the wall at the back
Was a brainwave with space for us all.

It's a wonderful room to relax in,
To read and to dream and to write
And fine birds with fine feathers fly down in all weathers
Affording me endless delight.

Note, the roof is constructed of K Glass
Opaque, through which no one can see
So I'm free to trade words with the bees and the birds
But the birds and the bees can't see me.

I've created a sports club for pigeons
Who peck at the windows for kicks.
They descend for their tea at a quarter to three
And they gather for cocktails at six.

Adam's Ale, it appears, is their favourite
The gutters hold ample supplies.
After drinks have been sipped, inhibitions unzipped,
It is time for high jinks in the skies.

There's a noisy ascent to the ridge crest
The ski school is soon in full swing
As they practice their skills, with a few nasty spills,
And prepare for the ultimate fling.

Now, the roofing bars act as the ski slopes,
They line up in turn at the top.
Some know just how to glide with their wings spread out wide
Others hurtle downhill and can't stop.

Then the fledglings fly off: for the jet-set
The evening has barely begun
They assemble with glee for the great apres-ski
And romance, on the wall, in the sun.

Pigeon courtship is simply enchanting,
He strokes her pink breast with his beak.
It's a matter of pride not to hurry his bride
As he flaunts his seductive technique.

Yet true love does not always run smoothly
And interests at times overlap.
For if A falls for B who is flirting with C
There are grounds for a serious scrap.

With the conjugal knot duly fastened
They snuggle up close for a rest
He will never abscond for his word is his bond
And he's promised to build her a nest.

It is quiet overhead in the winter
No pigeons to trigger my pen
But I know they'll be back when the sun changes tack
And the ink will be flowing again.

I am a Camellia

'Camellia Williamsii'
Or 'Brigadoon', that's me
I'm central in a brand new bed
The finest place to be.

I'm one of twenty flowering shrubs
Planted a year ago.
Some have ballooned to twice their size
But some, like me, are slow.

Although I started out quite small
My roots thrust down unseen
And overhead my stem grew strong
With leaves of lustrous green.

The lady who looks after us
Is not concerned with size.
She's taken quite a shine to me,
I see it in her eyes.

When days grew short and winds blew cold
And Jack Frost prowled at night
She dashed out with my overcoat
And buttoned me up tight.

The other shrubs made rude remarks
They called me 'Mummy's Pet'.
I kept my head and held my tongue
They ain't seen nothing yet!

And sure enough, in February,
I felt a surge of power
By March a mass of deep pink buds
Were bursting into flower.

Those buds became so burdensome
My arms began to ache,
At times I had to let them fall
Before they were awake.

Good will abounds around the bed
Since I put on a show.
Mahonia, who is very smart.
Now says I'm comme il faut!

I realise, in the summer months
When all my flowers have died
My neighbours will be gearing up
To blossom by my side.

My turn to compliment my friends,
Take pride in their display
For every plant, like every dog,
Must surely have its day.

The lady will be overjoyed
To see how fine they are.
I'll bide my time till Spring comes round
Then I shall be the star.

Golden Showers

'Golden Showers', you can't miss me, I'm first in the line
My continual blooms are exceedingly fine.
I start budding in May and flower through to the fall
When Jack Frost comes around and puts paid to us all.

I have grown very fast and have spread myself wide
So I may have frustrated the rose by my side.
She is thought to be strong and much taller than me
But she's lazy, bad tempered and French, c'est la vie!

She clings to the fence in a permanent sulk
She has named me, I hear. The Incredible Hulk.
It is best to ignore this unladylike sneer,
I'm in loco parentis to roses round here.

We were nine when we started but now we are eight
'Zepherine Drouhin' fell prey to a terrible fate.
She developed a virus, a sort of dry rot,
She was such a good neighbour, I miss her a lot.

They arrived one fine morning with barrows and boots
They examined the patient and dug up her roots.
There was shaking of heads as they wheeled her away
The Great Gap left behind is still with us to-day.

'Lady Hillingdon Climbing' lives down at the end
An unfortunate spot for my elegant friend
She was happy at first with her place in the row
And the sun gave her strength as she started to grow.

Then a bold 'Pittosporum' went crazy one night
Pushed her into the corner and banished her light.
Only one perfect bloom were we destined to see
As she vanished from sight from the sun and from me.

I've heard talk through the window which borders my head
About where they can find her a suitable bed.
The Great Gap has been broached as a new habitat
But I guess she'll have something to say about that!

Well, I've finished my piece and you'll hear me no more
For my friends have accused me of being a bore.
I shall keep my own counsel and bid you farewell
For each rose has a tale they are anxious to tell.

Madame Alfred Carriere

I hope you will not pass me by
Without a second glance
I'm Madame Alfred Carriere
My forbears hail from France.

I came to live by 'Golden Showers'
A bossy, macho rose.
He rambles on for endless hours
And gets right up my nose.

Without his unrestrained embrace
I would have made the grade
But leaning out across my face
He shoved me in the shade.

I have a noble pedigree
Second, I'm told to none.
But that is little use to me
Sequestered from the sun.

I should have been the best in show
A mass of scented bloom,
Not indisposed and lying low
Within a darkened room.

This will not be my Waterloo
My buds will stand and fight.
I'll find a way to guide them through
And steer them to the light.

There's wonderful support for me
From 'Breath of Life', close by.
She'll help my buds to struggle free
And point them to the sky.

So when they prune and cut us short
In Autumn or in Spring
Then 'Golden Showers' can list to port
And I shall have my fling.

Breath of Life

"What's in a name?" so Shakespeare boldly said
(We roses are well versed if not well read.)
"That which we call a rose would smell as sweet
By any other name." Well, what a cheat

To rearrange the facts to fit the play
We need to make a stand and have our say.
For every rose acquires a proper name
Each one unique, no character the same.

The older English rose is pure delight
Perfumes the day and lingers through the night.
While modern roses, though they may enthral
With new-found virtues, have no scent at all.

Roses may well embrace their names with pride
With history, poet or playwright by their side
My 'Breath of Life' means all the world to me
Without those wondrous words where would we be?

My days are spent encouraging my friends
Like "Madame Alfred Carriere" who depends
On my advice to help her find the sun
Since "Golden Showers" has had her on the run.

"A Shropshire Lad" spreads out his arm to hide
The space where "Zepherine Drouhin" lived and died.
My eager stems sometimes entwine with his,
I hoped for more, but no, so there it is.

A Shropshire Lad

Although I am 'A Shropshire Lad'
You will not find me there.
I flourish in a distant pad,
The Severn flows elsewhere.

I do not dwell near Ludlow town
Nor yet on Wenlock Edge
I thrive below a Southern Down
Beside a Hampshire hedge.

I climb with utmost ease and grace
Above the trellised wall
My peach-pink blooms have pride of place
The finest rose of all.

With rue my heart is laden
For golden friends I had,
For many a rose-lipt maiden
And many a lightfoot lad.

"By brooks too broad for leaping
The lightfoot boys are laid;
The rose-lipt girls are sleeping
In fields where roses fade."

I bow my head to 'Breath of Life'
Who grows abreast of me.
I fear she yearns to be my wife
But that will never be.

Sometimes the lady reads aloud
From Housman's tour de force
I own to feeling deeply proud
To share this Shropshire source.

Our guardian strolls, when day is spent,
Round every rose in sight.
She strokes our petals, breathes our scent
And bids us all "Good night."

Zepherine Drouhin

I'm sending this message by pigeon,
I hope he will forward it fast
After having a go on the ski slope below
He will drop it off as he flies past.

The lady with luck, will retrieve it
And read it aloud to my friends,
They will know I'm alive; how I came to survive
Then they' ll learn how the mystery ends.

I'll always remember the morning
They trundled me out through the gate.
For an age I was stuck in a dirty old truck
While they left me to ponder my fate.

Although I believed I was done for,
The night brought such torrents of rain
That my brave little root promptly started to shoot
I was back in the swim once again.

The gardener who came to collect me
Was staggered to find me alive.
"Finders Keepers," he said and he made me a bed
By his house where at last, I could thrive.

There's only one rose in the garden
It's me – and I'm having a ball.
There's no rivalry here, so I've nothing to fear
And I send my regards to you all.

Falstaff

If Will Shakespeare's your man then no doubt you're a fan
Of his plays, even now all the rage.
Henry IV, the first part, is a good place to start
Where my namesake looms large on the stage.

Sir John Falstaff, the pal of the wayward Prince Hal,
Who his Highness refers to as Jack,
Is a thorn in my side, robbing folk far and wide
With a perilous penchant for sack.

'Tis a poser: who knows how a beautiful rose
Should have come by this reprobate's name
And I need to unearth any relevant worth
That might help me to blot out the shame.

Though there's little to praise in his infamous ways
He has humour and wit, you' ll agree.
He will often amaze with a neat turn of phrase
And his talent endears him to me.

'Breath of Life' was ill-starred when she challenged the bard
How uncivil to take him to task.
'Twould be wiser if she had discussed it with me
As the only descendant to ask.

We came close to a row but we're friends again now
There is peace in these parts for a spell
But my gallant red rose keeps them all on their toes
And I'm Happy as Larry: All's Well...!

Sombreuil

A True Story

Sombreuil, a lovely gentle name
And few would ever know
The dreadful past from whence it came
In days of long ago.

In France, the Revolution took
The country to its knees.
The King deposed and brought to book,
The nobles, by degrees

Were seized, imprisoned, helpless, while
The Reign of Terror loomed.
The blameless held without a trial
And rich and poor were doomed.

Among the throng, with naught to plead,
Blue blood their only crime,
The Governor of Les Invalides
Was forced to bide his time.

The Count Sombreuil, for it was he,
Pined for his daughter fair.
The bold lass stole the gaoler's key
Her father's fate to share.

Held captive now, this brave young maid
Dreamed up a daring plan.
Success would mean a masquerade
As peasant girl and man.

She donned the Cap of Liberty,
The famous Bonnet Rouge.
Thus camouflaged could oversee
The final subterfuge.

She sought a prisoner who had died,
Half buried in the mud
Extracting from his wounded side
A cup of wine-red blood.

She faced her captors, bold as brass,
Her father standing by.
"We are not of the ruling class
As I will testify.

My father is no aristo,
We hate them all, I swear.
Attend and I will prove 'tis so,
Deny me if you dare."

Raising aloft her blood-filled prize
She drank for all to see.
The guards shrank back with haunted eyes
"Come, drink," she said "with me."

The gaolers hid, no volunteers
Could anywhere be found
And at this sight their blood-stained spears
Did rattle to the ground.

"Sombreuil is innocent!" they cried
Their panic plain to see.
Bolts drawn, keys fumbled, gates flung wide
And man and maid were free.

This demoiselle, the people's friend,
Her exploits noised abroad,
Helped bring The Terror to an end
And order was restored.

Her fame lives on, it does not fade,
A loyal admirer chose
To dedicate to this fair maid
Sombreuil, a perfect rose.

'Rosette-shaped blooms of creamy-white'
Describes me to a T.
'Refinement, charm' all bring to light
My bourbon ancestry.

Though fragrant scent and fan-shaped spread
Enhance the trellised wall,
This secret, safe inside my head
Delights me most of all.

So, if perchance, the wind and rain
Should tear my rose apart
You'll find the faintest blood-red stain
Deep down within my heart.

Iceberg

I'm a jolly Floribunda
I'm an enterprising rose
I'm a mountaineering wonder
With my tiny tendril toes.

I can ramble up the palings
Where no other rose has been,
Then I hang around the railings
To survey the local scene.

'Golden Showers' thinks I'm a vandal
But he's jealous of my height
And my neighbours love the scandal
I regale them with each night.

Fragrant friends keep me in clover,
For I have no scent myself.
I'm a closet Casanova
Sitting firmly on the shelf.

There are many I could mention
But 'Sombreuil' is Number One.
She enjoys my full attention
As I shield her from the sun.

She is such a pretty lady
And her hold on me is strong.
'Falstaff' says her past is shady
But I think he's got it wrong

I can see the beech-clad glory
Of the Hangers on the hill.
Gilbert White has told their story
And his spirit lingers still.

At night I dream of things unseen
And secrets no-one knows,
And wonder what I might have been
If I were not a rose.

Lady Hillingdon

Lady Hillingdon here, what a terrible year
Since I came to my personal plot.
I was eager to shine in this corner of mine
An extremely desirable spot.

I was doing quite well 'till disaster befell
In the shape of an evergreen shrub.
'Pittosporum', by name, he alone was to blame
For my downfall, the flightly young cub!

Surely everyone knows, if you're planting a rose
By a shrub, it needs plenty of space.
Not a neighbour whose breath nearly chokes you to death
With his foliage all over your face.

We were both a bit slow when we started to grow
Then my sidekick took off overnight.
He had been in cahoots with my burgeoning shoots
But by morning he'd stolen our light.

I tried hard to push through, which was all I could do
With no moon and no stars and no sun.
There was just about room for one apricot bloom,
When that fell to the ground - there were none.

Conversations abound, when the lady comes round,
About having my quarters assessed.
It' s a problem, I know, so I plan to lie low,
Keep my head down and hope for the best.

Calling all Roses by Golden Showers

Look out my friends, she's here again
Armed with her notebook and her pen.
Straighten your shoulders, raise your head,
Make sure your leaves are nicely spread.
Put out more buds to catch the eye
To please her as she passes by.

We ought to mind our P's and Q's
When spelling out the garden news
For though the words stay in our head
She knows exactly what we've said.
So, should we figure in her book,
It matters how we sound and look.

Our readers, as they turn the page,
May find a flower that's all the rage.
Then, if they like our stories too,
They'll choose a rose like me or you.
It's up to us to give our best
And let the lady do the rest.

Epilogue

November now; most roses are asleep
But 'Golden Showers' has tiny buds that creep
Towards the window where I stand and gaze
At barren stems, longing for warmer days.

Yet 'Breath of Life' is loath to say goodbye
Thrusting one final flower towards the sky
While lusty 'Falstaff', not to be outdone,
Has sired two bairns to catch the wintry sun.

A distant flash of yellow through the gloom
Shows brave 'Mahonia' bursting into bloom.
Sweet-smelling buds on curving arms raised high
To cheer the soul and captivate the eye.

I find 'Camellia' hanging on the brink
Of giving birth, a warm, expectant pink.
Her early tight-packed flowers may well be lost
Unless I move to guard her from the frost.

'The Pilgrim' rose, severely pruned and shorn
Clings closely to the wall below the lawn.
A riot of yellow, constant through the year;
A poet? If so, he does not bend the ear.

Hope springs eternal, signs are all around
While hidden powers work wonders underground
And though this weary world has lost its way
The garden lives to bloom another day.